Silver
Jubilee Year

A Complete
Pictorial Record

SILVER JUBILEE

JUBILEE

A COMPLETE PICTURE

SILVER JUBILEE

VER
E YEAR

TORIAL RECORD

Photography©Serge Lemoine and Press Association.

First published in Great Britain in 1977 by
Colour Library International Ltd.,
80-82 Coombe Road, New Malden, Surrey, England

Separation by La Cromolito, Milan, Italy.

Printed by INGRA Trento, Italy.

Bound by L.E.G.O. Vicenza, Italy.

Display and text filmsetting by
Focus Photoset Ltd.,
90-94 Clerkenwell Road, London, England.

ISBN 0 904681 56 4

Silver Jubilee Year

A Complete Pictorial Record

by Serge Lemoine

Produced by

Ted Smart & David Gibbon

COLOUR LIBRARY INTERNATIONAL

CONTENTS

Her Majesty the Queen's Silver Jubilee visits start on the Island of Tonga

The Queen and Prince Philip paid a brief one-day visit to the Kingdom of Tonga on Monday 14th February where they were greeted by His Majesty King Taufa'ahau Tupou IV, GCVO., KCMG., KBE., and Her Majesty Queen Halaevalu Maca'aho. Thousands of schooolchildren and well wishers lined the streets to cheer the Queen during her short drive from the docks to the Royal Palace.

After a private conversation and an exchange of gifts with the King of Tonga, the Queen and Prince Philip were treated to a Tongan Feast at Mala'e Pangai.

The feast included roast wild pigs, lobsters and exotic fruits. The guests had to squat, as the local tradition demands, but a small seat was provided for the Queen. After the Tongan Feast, The Queen and Prince Philip, with the King and Queen of Tonga, watched traditional Tongan dancing for two hours.

The King of Tonga had embarked on a rigorous diet prior to the Queen's visit, reducing his massive weight by 17 stones to a mere 28 stones.

It was Her Majesty's third visit to the Kingdom of Tonga since her accession to the Throne.

The Queen *left* in a happy, smiling mood on the lawns of the Royal Palace.
The Queen and the King of Tonga *top right* during the Tongan feast at Mala'e Pangai.
The Queen and Prince Philip with the King of Tonga in front of the Royal Palace *bottom right.*
The King and Queen of Tonga welcoming Her Majesty and Prince Philip *overleaf* as they disembark from the Royal Yacht Brittania at Nuku'alofa.

Fiji

The Queen's Speech at Albert Park, Suva, 16th February, 1977.

Chiefs and People,

You have received me as Queen of Fiji with the traditional and deeply impressive ceremony of welcome and I thank you for it. Each time I have seen it performed I have been made more conscious of its meaning and significance. It confirms those valued links, forged more than one hundred years ago, between Fiji and my family.

It is almost as if the very distance we live apart draws us closer when we meet, and just as my family is deeply conscious of your trust and affection for the Crown, so we for our part have the warmest feelings for the people of Fiji.

Similar bonds of respect and affection have held Fiji and the United Kingdom together in a friendship that has matured over the years until the present day when they meet as fellow members of the Commonwealth at Commonwealth meetings, and at other great International Councils of the World.

Here the qualities of justice, harmony and tolerance are valued, and by your example you can show how much can be achieved when different races live and work together pooling their talents and resources for the good of all.

We are indeed happy to be with you and are much looking forward to our visit to the North.

Thank you for the warmth of your welcome.

May God bless you all.

The Queen and Prince Philip were welcomed to Fiji by hundreds of small craft escorting the Royal Yacht Brittania into Suva harbour.

In accordance with ancient custom, before the Queen could set foot on Fiji as Queen of the island she had to be granted permission by the Chiefs, who came aboard Brittania to perform the ritual ceremony.

During the ceremony the Queen was presented with a 'Tumba' –a whale tooth. Before the days of the great whalers the Tumba was carved in wood.

Her Majesty delivers her speech *left* to the people of Fiji at Albert Park, Suva.

The Queen performs the ritual ceremony *above* of drinking a bowl of N'gona, which is made from the crushed roots of the pepper tree. It is understood that this particular drink is, to say the least, something of an acquired taste!

Prince Philip's turn *above* to drink the N'gona. Sheltering from the rain *below* the Queen and Prince Philip at the unveiling of a statue of Ratu Sir Lala Sukuna, ex-Speaker and Member of the Legislature, and uncle of Ratu Sir Kamisese Mara, the present Prime Minister.

A display of local dances at Albert Park *left* performed by members of the four main communities: Fijian, Indian, Chinese and European, is watched by a relaxed, and obviously happy, Queen.

The Queen and Prince Philip touring the sports ground *right* at Labasa, where they attended a garden party and watched Fijian and Indian dancing.

Some of the Fijian dancers *below* who performed for the Queen at Labasa.

New Zealand

Her Majesty the Queen, wearing the traditional Maori cape, *above* at the opening of the Royal New Zealand Polynesian Festival at Rugby Park, Gisborne.

The Queen declares open the Royal New Zealand Polynesian Festival at Gisborne, Saturday, 26th February, 1977.

Archdeacon Ihaka, Mr Ngata,

E Te Iwi Rau Rangitira Ma Tena Koutou Tena Koutou Tena Koutou Katoa,

Thank you for the welcome you have given us on behalf of the host tribes of this district, and the tribal groups from "the four winds". They represent the many canoes here today, whose names are preserved in the traditional songs, dances and chants which have been performed in my honour.

Whenever we have visited New Zealand, the Maori people have greeted us with loyalty and goodwill. We have the happiest memories of the welcome we were given here at Gisborne in 1970. Since then many of your elders have gone to join their ancestors and it is right that they too should be remembered here today. We remember also Mrs Ngarimu.

Archdeacon Ihaka. I congratulate you and your Committee on what has been done to conserve and develop Maori and Polynesian culture. These efforts will help to give the Maori and Polynesian people a balance and a consciousness of their identity which, in the face of the growing complexities of modern life, are good things to have. Mr Ngata. You have spoken in moving terms of the contribution made by Maori leaders in the past to increase understanding and goodwill between Maori and Pakeha and of the gallantry and self sacrifice shown by Maori soldiers.

A Jubilee, by tradition, is a time not only to rejoice but also to take stock. For the Maori people the last 25 years have brought great changes and in particular a shift from rural to urban living. This presents a challenge and in meeting it there is much to be learnt from the Maori of old. When looking to the future he looked also to the past for guidance.

Occasions such as this Festival remind us of the old and trusted values, which are still valid. They also provide an opportunity to share knowledge and experience for the common good. As the Maori proverb says "by your basket and by my basket will the visitors be contented".

People from all parts of the Pacific region now live in New Zealand, and many Island groups are taking part in this Festival. An increasing number of those of European origin also, now wish to know more of the ways and traditions of Maoris and Polynesians.

With a population woven from many strands New Zealanders have the opportunity to create a climate in which the virtues of many cultures can be shared by all. Differences will always arise, but these should not be reasons for discouragement. They should be taken as opportunities to understand better other people's points of view. In this way "May peace and harmony prevail".

It is in this hope that I have great pleasure in declaring open the Royal New Zealand Polynesian Festival of 1977.

The Queen accepts the traditional Maori challenge *right*. Before this ceremony is completed she cannot, by right, enter the Maori territory as their Queen.

Still wearing the traditional Maori cape *below* the Queen watches dancers from the Polynesian islands.

Some of the dancers *centre right* who provided entertainment for the Queen and Prince Philip.

After the dancing the Queen walked among the performers *bottom right* and talked to several of them.

Pages 20 to 23. During her two-week visit to New Zealand the Queen went on more than a dozen walkabouts, to the great delight of the cheering crowds. It was Her Majesty's express wish that such walks should take place so that the people would have a chance to see her at close range. These pictures illustrate two of these walks.

The Queen met with varied weather during her New Zealand tour. It was fine but chilly *left* as she drove among the crowds in a Land Rover.

During her short stop at Blenheim *centre left and right* she was met by heavy rain but still insisted on meeting the crowds massed at the airport.

It was fine weather again for the Queen and the waiting crowds during her visit to Greymouth *left*.

And again fine weather *above* for a day at the races in New Plymouth.

The Queen's Opening of Parliam

Wellington, Monday, 28th February, 1977.

Honourable Members of the House of Representatives.

I am delighted once more to be among my people in New Zealand to mark the twenty-fifth anniversary of my Accession.

I am, as always, greatly touched by the respect paid to the role of the Crown in your Constitution and by the warm regard shown for me personally.

My husband and I much appreciate the arrangements which my Ministers have made to enable us to tour New Zealand extensively so that we can meet as many people as possible.

I have looked forward to exercising my prerogative of opening this special second session of the thirty-eighth Parliament so that I can join, with the elected representatives of my people, in celebrating the 25 years of my reign. A jubilee, however, ought to be an occasion for looking towards the future as well as for looking back at the past.

The date of my Accession on 6 February coincided with Waitangi Day, so named by my Government as a lasting commemoration of the Treaty on which New Zealand's multi-cultural society is founded. This is, for me, a happy reminder of the lasting links between the Crown and the Maori people.

During these last 25 years New Zealand, like so many other countries, has experienced far-reaching developments in material terms and social change. The Government will meet the challenges and opportunities offered by this rapid evolution.

My Ministers believe they must create an environment in which individuals can choose their own roles and develop their particular talents provided that in doing so they do not infringe the rights of others. To promote true equality of opportunity the Government introduced at the end of the last session of Parliament a Bill to create a Human Rights Commission. My Ministers regard this as a measure of social as well as constitutional importance.

In the present situation, my Ministers are tackling the more immediate problems of inflation, growth, and stability, and are determined to devise policies which will:
promote greater production;
further restore business confidence;
minimise unemployment;
increase the earnings of exports from farming, fishing, and manufacturing;
develop the energy resources of the country;
continue, as appropriate, price and income control measures as necessary counterparts of each other; and
create harmonious industrial relations.

All these objectives will be sought within the context of providing incentives and rewards for productivity and thrift, conserving the nation's indigenous wealth, and preserving the natural environment.

My Ministers will also bring forward measures to cope with problems resulting from longer term trends such as rapid urbanisation linked with increased

Speech at the ent in New Zealand

industrialisation, the changing population structure, the increasing diversity of ethnic and cultural groups, and the emergence of a multi-cultural society with plural values. These policies will be formulated in line with the firm belief of my Ministers that the family unit is the continuing basis of New Zealand society.

My Ministers see New Zealand as a Pacific nation–in an increasingly interdependent world. The Government regards the South Pacific as a region of immediate New Zealand interest and will work with other independent and self-governing states of the region for mutual progress and welfare. The Government will continue to work for harmonious relations with all states and attaches particular importance to the Commonwealth and the United Nations as instruments towards this end.

The extension of trade–by diversifying products and services, attaining new markets and seeking to improve access to well-established ones–will continue to be a major aim of my Government's foreign policy. An equally important aim is the maintenance of close links for collective defence with New Zealand's traditional allies, of which the ANZUS Pact is the keystone.

The future may seem more complex or less clear than it was a generation ago, but I am sure that this will in no way inhibit the constructive spirit or impair the resolve of this young nation which believes in itself and can look forward to the future with confidence.

Honourable Members of the House of Representatives, I am grateful for the opportunity of being able to address you today as legislators who have successfully blended old and traditional forms with new institutions and practices.

A feature of the constitutional development of New Zealand has been the close identification of the Sovereign with the nation. In 1974 I gave my assent to an Act which defined the Royal Style and Titles in relation to New Zealand.

In line with this development my Ministers will introduce at this session a Bill to provide for the elevation of the Public Seal to the title of "The Seal of New Zealand" and to make amendments to the New Zealand statutes and those United Kingdom statutes in force in New Zealand which authorise the use of existing Seals.

The Seal of New Zealand will be used to execute New Zealand documents which at present pass under either the Public Seal or one of the United Kingdom seals. Thus I, as your Sovereign, will in future use The Seal of New Zealand on all such documents.

I note with appreciation that my Ministers intend, at the third session of this Parliament, to promote legislation establishing The Queen Elizabeth II National Trust which will commemorate my Silver Jubilee. The Trust is designed to ensure that sufficient open space is provided for the needs of New Zealanders.

I pray that the highest principles will continue to influence your deliberations and that the blessing of Almighty God rest upon your counsels.

Overleaf. A solemn and dignified occasion as Her Majesty, as Head of the Commonwealth, presides over the opening of a new session of Parliament in Wellington, New Zealand. Also present is His Royal Highness the Duke of Edinburgh.

More 'meet the people' walks in New Zealand,
and perhaps one of the most attractive dresses
worn by the Queen during Silver Jubilee Year.

**The Queen's Speech at Parliamentary
Reception, Canberra
Tuesday, 8th March, 1977.**

Mr Prime Minister, Mr Whitlam,
Mr Anthony,

Thank you all for your kind and generous remarks. As you may suppose, it is a great pleasure for me as Queen of Australia to be welcomed here at Parliament House in my Silver Jubilee year by the leaders of the three principal political parties of Australia.

It is one of the hall marks of the Parliamentary system, first developed at Westminster, that the leaders of opposing parties can join together on such occasions, without in any way diminishing the vigour or even the rancour of debate which takes place on others! So may it always be!

Last time I was in Australia, just three years ago, the uncertainties of politics in quite another part of the world forced me to cut short my visit. They also prevented me from returning, as I had hoped and planned to do, to visit South Australia, Western Australia and the Northern Territory. As we all know nothing is certain in this world so let me just say that I am looking forward this time with rather more confidence and a great deal of pleasure to visiting all six States and the Northern Territory.

Meanwhile it is very nice to be in Canberra again! We first came here together 23 years ago, long before there was a lake and when the capital was described as "seven suburbs in search of a city". That city has now been found and it is one of charm and character; it has become worthy of the nation.

The changes elsewhere in Australia since 1954 have been just as remarkable and during my five previous visits I have been able to watch the progress made with interest and admiration. It has been plain to see in all fields of Australian life, in commerce and

's Speech to
ralia

industry, in agriculture, science, technology and the arts.

But if much has changed there is something that has remained the same. If I had to find one word to describe it it would be "vitality".

This is a land of opportunity and not just a place where people come to make money and go away to spend it, but where they come to put down roots for themselves and to invest in the future for their families. That is why during the last quarter of a century almost 3 million people from more than 50 nations have come here to be Australians. They have added much to the richness and diversity of Australian life.

Mr Prime Minister, we look forward to welcoming you in June for the Jubilee celebrations in London and for your first meeting of Commonwealth Heads of Government. I think you will enjoy this occasion when so many leaders from all over the world and not least those from newly independent countries of the South Pacific to which the Leader of the Opposition has referred meet to exchange ideas and friendship.

I know you will also sense that Australia has a special place in the hearts and minds of the British people.

I have always found choosing names for racehorses a fascinating business. I shall particularly enjoy picking a name for your most welcome "gift horse"! With a sire called "Without Fear" and trying to find something with Australian connotations there should be plenty of scope!

I thank you and all Australians for this imaginative and exciting Jubilee gift.

And thank you, all three, once again for your welcome. We are delighted to be in Australia and are looking forward very much to our visit and to meeting Australians in every state, to meeting old friends and to making new ones.

During her tour of Australia the Queen was met by a group of Girl Guides on her arrival in Brisbane *left,* and later walked through the streets *above left* accompanied by the Lord Mayor, Alderman F.N. Sleeman.

Her Majesty pictured *above* during the Government Reception in Canberra.

The Queen meets the people during a walkabout in Freemantle, Western Australia *above*, and attends a children's rally *left* in Royal Park, Melbourne.

Accompanied by the Duke of Edinburgh, the Queen in Darwin *right* where she watched a Northern Territory Football League match between St. Mary's and Waratahs.

At a reception *above* of State Royal
Visit officials at Government House in
Hobart, Tasmania.

The Queen arriving *left* at North
Hobart Oval to attend the Tasmania
Military Tattoo.

Papua New Guinea

Her Majesty at a State dinner *left* at the Papua Hotel in Port Moseby.

Canoe racing at Alotan *above* watched by the Queen and the Duke of Edinburgh from the mv Tari.

A spectacular Papuan costume *right* at a 'people's welcome' to the Queen and Prince Philip in Port Moseby.

Ghana and the Ivory Coast

Previous page. While Her Majesty was visiting Australia, Prince Charles went to Ghana in March. In Kumasi he was guest of honour at a Durbar *left,* a gathering of the Ashanti Chiefs who only attend Durbars to greet great leaders or for councils of war.

The Durbar ceremony *top right* at Kumasi.

Prince Charles watching the ceremony *bottom right* from the shade of the Royal Dais.

This page. Students of the Achimota school provided entertainment *left top* for their royal guest.

The Prince was received *left centre* by the President of Ghana, General Acheapong, who presented him with a book of his speeches.

In Accra, Prince Charles presided over the passing out ceremony *left bottom* of cadets of the Ghanaian army and later posed with them for the offficial picture.

Prince Charles observing the playing of the National Anthems *above* on his arrival at the Achimota school.

The Chiefs with the Prince at the ceremony at the Achimota school *right.*

A group of beautiful girls *overleaf* from the Ivory Coast, their dresses decorated with his picture, await the arrival of the Prince at the airport.

After a cruise around the harbour installations in Abidjan, Prince Charles was entertained at an informal lunch at the Yacht Club *left*.

In Ghana, the Prince was made a local Chief by other Ghanaian Chiefs *below* and appeared to enjoy wearing the unusual robes of his new office.

The Queen and Princess Anne *overleaf* at the Easter service at St. George's Chapel, Windsor, soon after the announcement that the Princess would be expecting her first baby–and Her Majesty's first grandchild–in November.

The Badminton Horse Trials

Each year during the month of April, the Queen and her family attend the world famous Badminton Horse Trials, the most important three-day event meeting in the British calendar.

It is for the Queen an occasion to relax and enjoy her love of horses and, during the last five years, a chance to watch her daughter and son-in-law compete with the cream of international riders.

The Badminton Horse Trials are held on the land of the Duke of Beaufort, a long time friend of the Royal Family, and each year attract over a quarter of a million spectators. On cross-country day, usually held on a Saturday, The Queen and her family have an early lunch, and then drive in Land Rovers to several points on the course to follow the competition. They have at their disposal several horse carts to give them vantage points all along the course. Also at their disposal in each horse cart, but hidden from the public, are portable TV sets which allow them to follow the entire competition all the time.

The Queen and her family usually arrive on the Thursday and stay until the final show jumping on Sunday afternoon. Graciously, Her Majesty presents the cup to the winners late on Sunday afternoon in the main jumping arena.

The Badminton Horse Trials are a great favourite with the crowds who also find plenty of shops and catering facilities at their disposal.

The Queen, with The Queen Mother and Princess Margaret follow the competition on cross-country day *above* from a horse cart on the course.

The Queen, with Prince Edward, Viscount Linley, Lady Sarah Armstrong Jones and the Duke of Beaufort, at the veterinary inspection *right* on the last day of the trials.

The Queen and Princess Margaret *below* with the Duke of Beaufort's hounds.

Wearing tweeds, the Queen and the Queen Mother at the
inspection *right* prior to the cross-country event.

The Queen with Prince Edward, the Queen Mother, Viscount Linley, Lady Sarah Armstrong Jones and the Duke of Beaufort at the inspection before the cross-country event. Later, in order not to disturb other spectators, the Queen and the Queen Mother knelt on the grass with the Duke of Beaufort, by the water jump on the cross-country course *left and above*.

Overleaf. President Carter and President Giscard d'Estaing, in London for the Downing Street Summit, meet the Queen in the Blue Drawing Room at Buckingham Palace.

Pages 58 and 59. From the left, Pierre Trudeau (Canada), Takeo Fukada (Japan). Princess Margaret, James Callaghan, Prince Charles, Giscard d'Estaing (France), The Queen, The Queen Mother, President Carter (USA), Giulio Andreotti (Italy), Prince Philip and Helmut Schmidt (West Germany) in the Blue Drawing Room at Buckingham Palace when the Queen entertained the seven world leaders—in London for the two-day Downing Street Summit talks—to dinner.

The Royal Windsor Horse Show

The Royal Windsor Horse Show provides Prince Philip with an ideal opportunity to take part in the sport at which he now excels–carriage driving. The Prince takes the sport very seriously and wears a special outfit for the dressage, and a more relaxed style for the cross-country event. At one stage he had to negotiate a very tricky up-hill obstacle which required a considerable amount of skill and courage. He came through it brilliantly –and the Queen's smile clearly shows her relief.

The Queen's
Church of

The Queen's Speech at the Opening by Her Majesty of the Church of Scotland General Assembly on Tuesday, 24th May, 1977.

Right Reverend and Right Honourable,

Today, I am reminded of my previous visits to the General Assembly in 1960 and 1969. The memory of the welcome I received then made me resolve to be in Edinburgh during my Silver Jubilee Year as Queen at a time when I could once again attend your deliberations.

I have always followed the Assembly's work with close interest. The Lord High Commissioner has reported to me on the conclusion of each year's proceedings, and because this year I cannot be with you for the whole period, I have appointed the Earl of Wemyss and March, who is well known to you, to that office.

Right Reverend Moderator. I congratulate you on your election to the Chair of the Venerable Assembly. Fathers and Brethren, since the General Assembly last met many Ministers and Office Bearers have died. We remember them with gratitude and affection. Their influence, devotion and example will be with you as you address yourselves to your duties.

Fathers and Brethren pray be seated.

Twenty-five years ago I took a solemn oath to preserve and uphold the rights and privileges of the Church of Scotland. That solemn pledge I gladly reaffirm in your presence today.

During those twenty-five years I have seen at first hand much of the life and witness of the church at home and overseas. I am particularly glad, therefore, that representatives of the sister churches from developing countries in Africa and Asia are here today. They share the commitment of the Church of Scotland to seek peace and unity. They have done much for this cause which is all the more urgent today for the relief of racial and social tensions.

I am happy to have this opportunity to express my appreciation and admiration to you and to them directly.

Speech to the Scotland

During these same years this country has passed through very difficult times. The aftermath of the Second World War and the dramatic and swiftly changing circumstances that implied, has demanded a lengthy process of readjustment.

Much has been achieved but continued courage and perseverance are called for! And let us always remember that along with the difficulties there are great advantages. These Islands remain rich in material resources as new discoveries of coal, gas and oil have shown us. But these are finite and we must use them well and wisely.

But the greatest strength of any nation is in its human and spiritual resources. Christians everywhere are sustained and inspired by the ideal of the brotherhood of man and the commandment to love one another. They can set an example of service and self sacrifice, of reconciliation and unity, so as to make the world a better place for all.

For the people of this country which has achieved so much, there remains a powerful underlying sense of community and of direct links with generations past and still to come. In this fast changing temporal world, it is the task of the Church, by fresh inspiration and new understanding, to awaken and renew this sense of common stewardship.

Over the centuries perhaps the greatest moments in the history of our country have been in times of great adversity when the nation has stood alone, when we have been faced by the threat of more powerful material forces, but have been sustained by the strength of our own moral and spiritual conviction. Under God's will, we can still achieve that truer greatness in our own generation. For it is part of the Christian message that "time and chance happeneth to all men."

Opportunity lies with each and every generation in the circumstances of its day provided it acts with faith, courage and perseverance.

Fathers and Brethren. I pray most heartily that God's blessing may attend your deliberations.

After the informality of Glasgow and Perth, pageantry
caught up with the Queen when she arrived in Edinburgh.
Under misty skies, in front of thousands of people, the
massed bands of Pipes and Drums Beat the Retreat.
At St. Giles' Cathedral Her Majesty was met by a Guard
of Honour from the Scottish Regiments.

Overleaf
The Queen arriving in Scotland at the
start of her Silver Jubilee visit.

A patriotic Pekingese among the flag-waving crowds *above* in Perth, awaiting the arrival of the Queen.

During her Silver Jubilee tour of Scotland the Queen planted a tree *right* at Camperdown Park, Dundee.

Her Majesty at a Jubilee show at King's Theatre, Glasgow *left,* and examining *above* a model of the Argyll and Sutherland Highlanders' mascot which was presented to her as a Silver Jubilee gift at the Palace of Holyroodhouse in Edinburgh. The presentation was made on behalf of the regiment by Col. C.P.R. Palmer.

On her Jubilee visit to Scotland, the Queen had a very full schedule to maintain. On the first day of her visit she walked among the crowds *left* in Glasgow and, on the same day, she met members *below* of the Glasgow Select football team when she visited Hampden Park to watch them play against an England XI in a match in aid of the Silver Jubilee Appeal.

Another walkabout, this time in Perth, *right* and a talk to some of the children *below right* when the Queen paid a visit to the Jack Lane Community Centre at Craigmillar, Edinburgh.

The Queen and Prince Philip drive
in the Scottish State Coach *above*
along the Royal Mile from
Holyroodhouse to St. Giles' Cathedral
and *right* the Queen Mother and
Prince Charles travel the same route
on the first day of the visit
to Edinburgh.

Her Majesty delivering her speech
above-the full text of which appears
on pages 62 and 63-to the dignitaries
of the Church of Scotland in
Edinburgh.

Overleaf. Wearing the robes of the
Order of the Thistle, the Queen,
Prince Philip, Prince Charles and the
Queen Mother leaving St. Giles'
Cathedral after a service for the
Order-of which the Queen is
Sovereign.

Her Majesty the Queen in the Scottish State Coach *left*.

The Queen and Prince Philip pictured *above* leaving St. Giles' Cathedral.

The Queen and the Duke of Edinburgh at a garden party they gave in the gardens of Holyroodhouse for the dignitaries of Edinburgh, at which Her Majesty spent nearly two hours with her guests.

Cups being presented by the Queen *right* to the winners of youth group displays at Meadowbank Stadium, Edinburgh.

The Royal Opera House, Covent Garden was the setting *below* for a
Gala Jubilee performance of opera and ballet attended by the Queen.

Her Majesty at the Royal Windsor Big Top Show *right top and bottom*
which was given in Billy Smart's Circus tent in Home Park.

Derby Day

The Queen and prince Philip assess the runners *above*.

From the Royal Box *far left* the Queen takes a keen interest in all the racing and, no doubt, in the general scene of excitement on Epsom Downs.

The Queen and the Queen Mother in the paddock *top left and left* assessing the entries for the 1977 Derby.

The finish of the 1977 Derby *centre left* which was won by The Minstrel.

Silver Jubilee Bonfire

On the 6th June, in Silver Jubilee Year, Her Majesty the
Queen lit a special Jubilee bonfire in Windsor Great park
which was the signal for a chain of similar bonfires to
be lit over the length and breadth of the country to herald
the start of the Silver Jubilee celebrations.

Jubilee

Day

The Gold State Coach, *pictured here and on the following two double pages* pulled by eight Windsor Greys, with the Queen and Prince Philip en route for St. Paul's Cathedral for the Silver Jubilee Thanksgiving Service.

eThanksgiving aul's Cathedral

Her Majesty the Queen and Prince Philip *above and right and following two pages* during the Silver Jubilee Thanksgiving Service in St. Paul's Cathedral.

Leaving St Paul's Cathedral after the service: *left* the Duke and Duchess of Kent and their children the Earl of St. Andrews, Lady Helen Windsor and Lord Nicholas Windsor. The group also includes Prince Michael of Kent, Princess Alexandra and Lord Mountbatten.

One of the undoubted highlights of Jubilee Day was the Queen's walk from St Paul's Cathedral to Guildhall, where she had lunch. Some of the happy scenes are shown here and overleaf as Her Majesty, accompanied by the Lord Mayor of London, Sir Robin Gillett, took rather longer than had been intended for the walk, due entirely to the enthusiasm of the people and the Queen's wish to meet and speak to them.

The Queen's Jubilee Luncheon

My Lord Mayor.

I have had the pleasure of being entertained here on many occasions and I can think of no better place in which to celebrate my Silver Jubilee, both as Queen and Head of the Commonwealth. Your welcome and your kind words in proposing my health are very much appreciated and the response to it by your guests has touched me deeply.

Guildhall, in the City of London, has seen many National and Commonwealth celebrations, but in all its long history it has never witnessed the presence of so many Commonwealth Heads of Government.

In the olden days Jubilees were celebrated at the Golden fiftieth year. The horns were sounded and a period of "rest, mercy and pardon" was proclaimed. There was a distinct sabbatical flavour about the proceedings. It is beginning to dawn on me that a Silver Jubilee is of a somewhat different nature! But if this is not exactly a period of rest for us, it is certainly one of refreshment and of happiness and satisfaction. And the best of it is that it is giving us the chance to meet so many people in so many countries of the Commonwealth, to renew old friendships and to make new ones. At the Silver Jubilee of 1935 and at my Coronation the Empire and the Commonwealth came to London: this time the travelling is in both directions and I think we can claim to be doing our fair share!

During these last 25 years I have travelled widely throughout the Commonwealth as its Head. And during those years I have seen, from a unique position of advantage, the last great phase of the transformation of the Empire into Commonwealth and the transformation of the Crown from an emblem of dominion into a symbol of free and voluntary association. In all history this has no precedent.

It is easy enough to define what the Commonwealth is *not*, indeed, this is quite a popular pastime! But from my own experience I know something of what it is. It is like an iceberg, except that it's not cold!

The tip is represented by the occasional meetings of the Heads of Government and by the Commonwealth Secretariat, but nine tenths of Commonwealth activity takes place continuously beneath the surface, and unseen. Cultural activities, professional,

Speech at the
at the Guildhall

scientific, educational and economic bodies have between them created a network of contacts within the Commonwealth which are full of life and much valued. And right at the base of the iceberg, the part which keeps the rest afloat is friendship and communication, largely in the English language, between peoples who were originally brought together by the events of history and who now understand that they share a common humanity.

I have also no doubt that, politically, the Commonwealth has something rare and valuable to offer. A capacity for enlightened tolerance, the ability to see things in a long term perspective, and the willingness to concede that there just may be another point of view. It has the strength to endure difference for the sake of basic identity and the courage to prefer compromise to conflict.

It was this political perception which originally prompted the unprecedented transformation of the British Empire into a Commonwealth, into a voluntary association of equal partners in which no one claims pre-eminence.

An association of countries like the Commonwealth that has this wisdom need have no fear for the future. Far from it, it can look forward with abounding hope, not only for its own well being, but also that its example may point the way for mankind.

At this moment of my Silver Jubilee, I want to thank all those in Britain and the Commonwealth who through their loyalty and friendship have given me strength and encouragement during these last 25 years.

My thanks go also to the many thousands who have sent me messages of congratulations on my Silver Jubilee, that and their good wishes for the future.

In these messages I have sensed a spirit of happiness, friendship and hope and the recognition that people are important as individuals and have a responsibility for each other. May that spirit stay with us when these celebrations are over.

My Lord Mayor. When I was 21, I pledged my life to the service of our people and I asked for God's help to make good that vow.

Although that vow was made "in my salad days when I was green in judgement" I do not regret nor retract one word of it!

The following two double pages show the scene in the Guildhall, when the Queen and other members of the Royal Family attended a luncheon given by the Lord Mayor.

The end of a glorious day

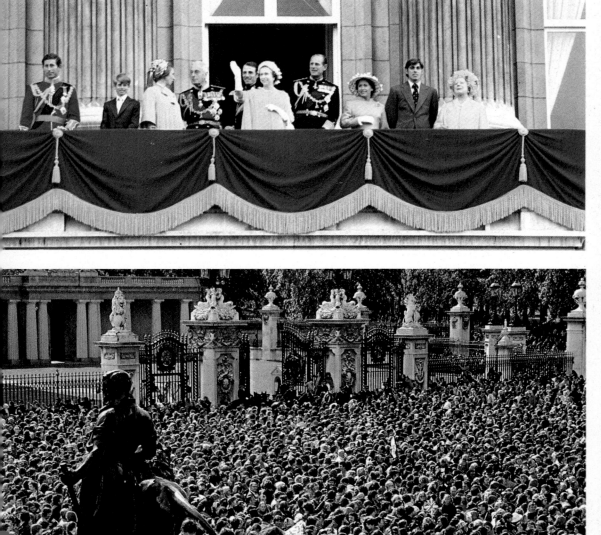

Fireworks c

ver London

A magnificent firework display *left* lights up the sky over the River Thames. The display, the largest ever seen in London, was watched by the Queen and members of the Royal Family, and by millions more on their television sets at home.

A flotilla of small craft surrounds the Royal Yacht Britannia in the Pool of London *below* as the Queen gives a luncheon party on board during her progress from Greenwich to Lambeth.

Trooping the Colour–Her Majesty's official birthday–is always held on a Saturday in June. It is a highlight of the British tourist season and a regular fixture in the Queen's year.

It is the most spectacular of the large number of military events she attends–from presenting colours to reviewing ships–and, as such, it requires a considerable amount of planning and preparation.

The Queen's mount has to be schooled for many weeks in advance in order to prepare it fully for its demanding task. A lady of the same build as the Queen stands in for her for much of the time but the Queen herself, during the last two weeks of training, spends at least an hour and a half each morning at the Buckingham Palace Mews accustoming herself to the side-saddle position traditionally used.

The ceremony of Trooping the Colour, which symbolises the special position of the regiments taking part, was first carried out in 1755 and has taken place fairly regularly since 1805. During the reign of Queen Victoria it was held to celebrate her actual birthday on the 24th of May. It is now held in the summer, on the Sovereign's 'official' birthday, because it is a sight that, not surprisingly, attracts thousands of tourists. Indeed, traffic congestion reached such a level that, in 1958, the day was changed to a Saturday.

Escorted by the Household Cavalry –the collective title given to the army's senior regiments–the Life Guards and the Blues and Royals–the Queen rides from Buckingham Palace, along the Mall to Horse Guards Parade.

In this, Jubilee, year, Prince Philip and Prince Charles rode alongside her, while the Queen Mother and other members of the Royal Family drove in carriages to the parade grounds.

After the ceremony the Queen returns to Buckingham Palace at the head of her troops, and at the gates of the Palace she salutes her escort.

Left. As on Jubilee Day, huge crowds waited in front of Buckingham Palace despite the torrential rain. Many in the crowds, including large contingents of foreign visitors, had waited for hours to catch a glimpse of the Queen and Prince Philip, and then of Prince Charles, leaving the Palace for Horse Guards Parade and then returning after the ceremony.

The crowds are always delighted to see the Queen riding back from the Trooping the Colour ceremony. This year many thousands of people, the biggest crowds seen since the Coronation, lined the Mall to see the Sovereign and to enjoy the pageantry of this great occasion *bottom left.*

The Queen and her family were on the balcony of Buckingham Palace *above* after the Trooping the Colour ceremony, to watch the fly-past by the RAF and to acknowledge the acclamation of the huge crowds massed in front of the palace gates. On the balcony, from left to right, are Prince Charles, Prince Edward, the Earl of St. Andrews, the Queen Mother, Lady Helen Ogilvy, Princess Anne, Princess Louise, Captain Mark Phillips, Her Majesty the Queen, Prince Philip and the Honourable Angus Ogilvy.

Crowds *right* outside Buckingham Palace eagerly awaiting the appearance, on the balcony, of the Queen and Prince Philip.

British Legion Parade

At the end of a busy week, Prince Charles reviewed, on Sunday morning, the veterans of the Royal British Legion on Horse Guards Parade. It was a solemn occasion with the veterans, men and women, proudly carrying their flags and parading in front of the Prince of Wales.

The Garter Ceremony

"The Most Noble and Amiable Company of St. George named the Garter" is the oldest order of Christian chivalry in Britain. It dates from April 23rd, 1349 when Joan, Countess of Salisbury, was dancing with King Edward III and her blue garter slipped to the floor. The King gallantly picked up the garter and, noticing his grinning courtiers, said: "Honi soit qui mal y pense–Shame on him who thinks evil of it".

The British have turned this casually flirtatious event into a ceremony that combines historical relic with contemporary patriotism and, each year, attracts a huge crowd.

Originally there were twenty-five Knights, including the Sovereign, but this number was increased in 1831 to allow the Prince of Wales and other members of the British and foreign Royal Families to be admitted. Before lunch, during a private ceremony in the Throne Room of Windsor Castle, the Queen invests the new Knights by buckling the blue and gold garter onto the left leg of the recipient. After lunch, and wearing the large blue garter insignia on the left breast, the

Knights of the order proceed to St. George's Chapel, preceded by the Military Knights of Windsor and various heralds. The procession is slow and members of the Royal Family are divided into two groups; first the Queen Mother escorted by the Prince of Wales, and then Her Majesty with Prince Philip at her side. A service is then held in St. George's Chapel following which the Queen and her family return to the castle in open carriages.

The Royal Progress England

The Queen acknowledges the salutes of ships in the Mersey *left* during her visit to Liverpool.

An evening of entertainment *middle right* for Her Majesty at the theatre in Manchester.

During her tour of the West Country, the Queen visited *right* St. Mawes, Cornwall.

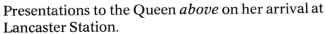

Presentations to the Queen *above* on her arrival at Lancaster Station.

In the West Country again, *right* the Queen and the Duke of Edinburgh driving up the course at the Devon and Exeter steeplechase meeting at Haldon racecourse.

In Nottinghamshire, the Queen was presented with a posy *below* at a gathering of children when she opened a new library in Mansfield.

The Queen and the Duke of Edinburgh in Ipswich, Suffolk, *bottom* during the Eastern England tour.

The Queen presented with flowers by children *above* during a walkabout in Mansfield, Nottinghamshire.

Still in Mansfield, the Queen is pictured *right* among the crowds.

At Butterley Hall, near Chesterfield,
the Queen was presented with a doll
overleaf as she walked among the
crowds in a sports field.

A young citizen *top left* makes a presentation to the Queen during her walkabout in Derby.

Derby is made a city *left*. The Queen presented a Charter conferring city status on Derby on the occasion of her Silver Jubilee visit.

Young residents greet Her Majesty in Dudley *above*.

A floral tribute is accepted *left* by the Queen from a group of youngsters in Birmingham's Victoria Square during her two-day tour of the West Midlands.

Wales

The Queen in Llandudno *left* during her Silver Jubilee tour of Wales.

A walkabout in Haverfordwest, Dyfed *middle left and bottom left.*

The 'leaning tower' *below* of Caerphilly Castle.

Twelve months old Karis Dillon with the Queen at Caerphilly Castle *right.* Karis was one of twenty-five children– one for each year of her reign– who greeted the Queen.

Her Majesty about to inspect *above* a Guard of Honour provided by a Welsh Regiment on her arrival at the Town Hall in Cardiff.

A great welcome *right* for the Queen as she enters Caerphilly Castle.

A great welcome *left and bottom left* for the Queen on her arrival at Caerphilly Castle–and a posy of flowers from two small children as she leaves.

The Queen walking among the people of Carmarthen *bottom centre* and waving to them *below* after signing the Golden Book of the town.

Her Majesty entering Llandaff Cathedral *top right,* where she arrived in an open coach and, later, leaving *bottom right* by car with posies of flowers in the rear window.

Fleet Review

Her Majesty reviewed the Fleet at Spithead and then visited Portsmouth where she is pictured with the crowd in Guildhall Square *above left* and on her walk *below left* from the Guildhall to the station.

The ship's company drawn up on the flight deck of the aircraft carrier Ark Royal *above* as the Royal Yacht Brittania passes during the Queen's Silver Jubilee Review of the Fleet.

The Royal Yacht Brittania passing along the lines of warships *right*. On board Brittania were the Queen, the Duke of Edinburgh and other members of the Royal Family.

On her walkabout *left and above* in the Commercial Road
shopping precinct in Portsmouth, the Queen was presented
with posies by local children.

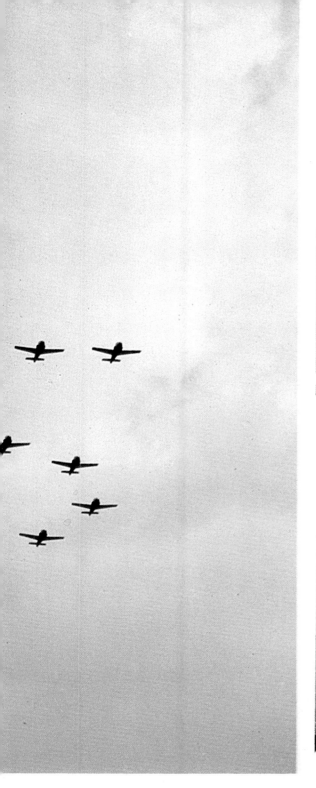

Royal Air Force Review

Jet Provost trainers fly *above left* in the form of a symbolic "25".

The Queen and the Duke of Edinburgh driving in an open field car along the lines of aircraft and crews *far left* on the occasion of the Silver Jubilee Review of the Royal Air Force at RAF Finningley.

Her Majesty presenting a new Queen's Colour *left* for the Royal Air Force.

A farewell wave from an aircraft of the Queen's Flight *above* as Her Majesty leaves after the review.

Prince Charles in Canada

In July, Prince Charles attended a ceremony to mark the
centennial of the signing of an Indian Treaty, in Calgary,
Canada. He was presented with ornamental Indian clothes
and head-dress–which he wore for the peace-pipe smoking
ceremony at Blackfoot Crossing.

The Queen
Norther

Thursday, 11th August, 1977.

This is the last day of my Jubilee visits around the United Kingdom and I am glad that it should be spent amongst the people of Northern Ireland who have suffered, and courageously borne, so much.

Mr Mayor, Mr Chancellor.

I am grateful to you both for your friendly welcome, for your hospitality and for this opportunity to speak to all the people of this Province. I am pleased to be able to do this from the University of Coleraine because it is here that young people come together to prepare themselves to play a full part in the future of this country.

How different this is from the image so many people have of what life is like here! They think only of separate and beleaguered communities living in fear and without hope. The atmosphere in this hall today shows just how wrong that image is.

It is eleven years since we were last here! During much of that time we have watched events with deep concern and sadness. No one could remain unmoved by the violence and the grief that follows it. But we have also watched with admiration the fortitude and resilience with which the challenge has been met.

The sufferings here have evoked sympathy and concern throughout the world and nowhere more than in the rest of the United Kingdom. To see such conflict taking place within our country emphasises the clear and continuing responsibility for us all to bring back peace and stability to this community.

During these last two days, I have met men and women from all walks of life, including

s Speech in n Ireland

many who have been directly affected by the violence. I have been encouraged by talking to widows who, despite their personal loss, look forward without bitterness to the time when peace will return. There are hopeful signs of reconciliation and understanding. Policemen and soldiers have told me of the real co-operation they are receiving. I have sensed a common bond and a shared hope for the future.

People, everywhere, recognise that violence is senseless and wrong and that they do not want it. Their clear message is that it must stop. And that is my prayer too. In this improving atmosphere those with different beliefs and aspirations understand that if this community is to survive and prosper they must live and work together in friendship and forgiveness. There is no place here for old fears and attitudes born of history, no place for blame for what is past.

It is to the future that we must look, for that is the most important concern for us and for our children. And I believe we can look to it with hope.

Every visitor here is surprised that normal life goes on! As word of this spreads abroad, investors, industrialists, and tourists will realise that this beautiful country and its diligent people have much to offer.

The aim of all, Government and people, must be to turn into reality our hopes for a peaceful and stable future and a better life for all. I believe the opportunity is there to be grasped.

I look forward to the day when we may return to enjoy with the people of Northern Ireland some of the better and happier times so long awaited and so richly deserved.

The last engagement carried out by Her Majesty the Queen during her Silver Jubilee tour of the United Kingdom was a visit to Northern Ireland on August 10th and 11th. She received a rapturous welcome, especially at the new University of Coleraine, where she delivered her speech to the people of Northern Ireland. An unexpected visitor, for a brief period, was Prince Andrew, who also received a warm personal welcome.

After lunch, and her speech, the Queen and Prince Philip attended a youth display and, later, a garden party, where they spent a considerable time talking to people from many different parts of the Province.

During her six week tour of the Pacific Islands and Australasia, the Queen once again used the Royal Yacht Brittania as her official residence. Brittania has, sometimes, been criticised as an unnecesary expense, but it has to be borne in mind that the yacht becomes more than just a floating palace; it serves the purpose of an office, the nerve centre of the Monarchy and, perhaps most important, British territory to which foreign heads of state and other dignitaries and officials can be invited for discussions, State banquets, and so on.

The Royal Yacht also provides accommodation and offices, often in cramped conditions, for the assortment of officials, policemen, pages, doctors, secretaries and servants who accompany the Queen on her voyages.

To set up this temporary residence the Queen requires a considerable amount–just over seven tons– of luggage which includes specially selected items from her wardrobe and, of course, all the jewellery appropriate for State Receptions and engagements. In addition, the Queen has to take with her many important papers plus just over a ton of silver-framed photographs and assorted presents.

Perishable items include fresh yoghurt, cream, milk, cheeses, cakes etc., and an assortment of wines–plus the inevitable Malvern water.

When Her Majesty boarded the Royal Yacht Brittania in Pago Pago, American Samoa, it took no less than seven lorries to transport the luggage from the special British Airways Super VC 10 to the yacht. The Queen's luggage is carried in huge mauve trunks with her name clearly printed on each one. Prince Philip's luggage is carried in separate trunks, as are the State Papers.

Photographs on pages:
34, 35, 36, 37, 38, 39, 56 & 57, 58 & 59, 60, 66 & 67, 68, 69, 70,
71, 80, 81, 84, 85, 86 & 87, 90 & 91, 102, 103, 104, 105,
108 & 109, 110 & 111, 112 (top and centre), 114, 115, 121
(bottom), 129 (centre left, top right and bottom right), 130,
131, 132 & 133, 134, 135, 136, 137, 142, 143, 144, 145, 146 and 147
supplied by the Press Association.

All remaining photographs are the copyright
of Serge Lemoine.